Copyright © 2018 by Vaag H. Durgarian

All rights reserved.

Published in Dubai, United Arab Emirates

ISBN 978-1-387-94709-6

Praise for

Vaag H. Durgarian's

The Map Is Not the Territory.
Leading Change In Multinational Corporations

„With constant disruption being the norm in the digital economy, managing change and getting colleagues onboarded for the transformation journey will be the key to success for established corporations. Vaag's topical book explores how corporations will need to reinvent and transform for this journey."
—Luka Mucic, Chief Financial Officer, SAP SE

„Change management is often viewed as an undesirable event originating from economic or political source forcing companies to deal with. Vaag's book demonstrates that companies must have a proactive approach, anticipate change and prepare for it. So, change management should give place to implementing change and leading change as it is brilliantly demonstrated in this book."
—Cedomir Nestorovic, Professor, ESSEC Business School

„This book really reflects strong experience in managing the change in different roles and

geographies which can be very useful during transformation strategy development and its implementation stages. Vaag touches deeply talent role in change management and helps to understand the process of transformation implementation in blue chip companies. I recommend this book to current and future leaders."
—Gregory Nazaryan, Regional Practice Leader, Stanton Chase

„Vaag has keen insight on the requirements on driving change management firsthand. He played a key part in the success of our global finance transformation which helped SAP achieve its modernized finance structure. Without the focus on change management, it's doubtful we could have achieved the final state in which we currently operate."
—Joel Bernstein, Chief Financial Officer of Global Customer Operations, SAP SE

That people perceive things differently is a given. Crucially, these perceptions often diverge from the reality of a situation. People think and act based on what I call the "map" of the reality, its likeness. However, the map does not always correspond to the "territory" of the reality, the facts on the ground.

Even in the best of cases, the map can only depict the topography of the territory. It can never take its place.

Fortunately, map-making, like leadership, has come a long way. To navigate the complexities of today's business world, it is critical to consistently enhance and update our map, make it as accurate as possible, as analogous to the territory as we can. A precise map, one based on facts, statistics and qualitative research, helps us refine our thoughts and actions and leads us down the right road.

Managing change in a multinational corporation is a formidable challenge. Today's companies enjoy unprecedented size and scope. Their large footprint comes complete with a multitude of viewpoints and experiences from people all over the world.

This book is a practical guide on how to manage change, particularly the people aspect of it, in a multinational corporation. Some of the new ideas introduced in this book deal with different levels of change impact on employees, the creation of strategy during transformation, delivering measurable positive experiences, and making transformation positive and sustainable for both the employees and the company.

It is intended as a practical guidance for senior and middle management and any team driving transformation in multinational corporations, as well as an additional literature for students studying change management discipline.

DEDICATION

This book is dedicated to all those who make the world and people around them better every day.

It would not have been possible without the support and encouragement of my family, Tatevik, Michelle, Gregory, and my parents.

CONTENTS

1. INTRODUCTION

Multinational corporations (hereinafter – MNC) have a rich history starting back in the 13th Century. It is hard to exaggerate their contribution to the world's growth, not only economically, but scientifically and culturally as well. Starting early 21st century, multiple forces and trends have encouraged MNCs to transform. This book is a simple receipt on how to manage changes coming from a transformation to reach intended objectives through keeping high employee engagement, retaining talents, and thus get sustainable lasting benefits. This book introduces ideas about different levels of impact of the change on employees, strategy during transformation, and that the quantity of positive change management activities ultimately turns into the quality.

2. MNC HISTORY AND SPECIFICS

MNCs are among the major institutions in the world. An estimate suggests that 250 MNCs possess/control a quarter of the world's assets which are involved in production, which is worth approximately US$5 trillion. Metrics of one MNC may be comparable to, or even greater than the yearly gross domestic product (GDP) of many countries. Sales revenues of Itochu Corporation's are higher than the GDP of Austria, while those of Royal Dutch/Shell are close to Iran's GDP. Due to their size, MNCs are likely to have a dominant position in those areas where trade is in the form of oligopoly, or not many companies manages the market share. Globally, the top five producers of cars and trucks manage around 65 percent of worldwide sales of those products. 40% of global oil market share is managed by the top five global oil corporations. 35% of chemical sector is managed by a small number of corporations. In the past MNCs were predominantly based in Western Europe, North America, and Japan, however currently they emerge in many other countries too. Regardless of their primary location, operations of MNCs span the globe. For example, ABB (a Swiss electrical engineering MNC) has operations in 140 countries. Royal Dutch/Shell explores for oil in 50 countries, refines in 34, and markets in 100. H.J. Heinz (a US food processing MNC) has presence on six continents. Cargill (a US's grain MNC) works in 54 countries. ICI (a Britain's chemical MNC) does manufacturing in 40 countries.

There are different definitions of MNCs, but for this book let us assume that MNC means a for-profit corporation with two characteristics:

- It does business in several countries outside the country of its origin; and

- Decisions by its management are made based, not on the situation in the country of its origin, but a bigger picture in the region where it operates.

MNCs can be public companies, with shares being traded at different stock exchanges. Any individual or company can buy those shared and become a minority shareholder of an MNC. Examples are Microsoft and DuPont. Or a MNC can be a private company. Private companies are usually owned by some undisclosed shareholders. Examples are Cargill, Dell, and PricewaterhouseCoopers. Private MNCs directly manage subsidiaries located in other countries. Public MNCs can do so via owning full or partial shares of subsidiaries located in other countries. There are different levels of control and management of country subsidiaries by the headquarters.

History of MNCs starts from Knights Templar (Templars or Order). Templars were among the wealthiest organizations in the Western Christian world. That organization appeared during Middle Ages and existed for a couple of hundred years. The Roman Catholic Church endorsed Knights Templar around 1129. The Templars managed a large economic and financial infrastructure on the territories controlled by the Roman Catholic Church. In 1150 the Order started to create letters of credit for pilgrims who would go to the Holy Land. Pilgrims used to leave their valuables with a local Templar deposit before the start of the journey. They used to get documents which specified the value of their deposit. After the arrival to the Holy Land they used that document to retrieve their funds in an amount of treasure of equal value. Such a system was innovative and can be related to a very early form of banking, and may have been the first formal system to support the use of cheques. This helped make pilgrims a less attractive target for thieves. The first headquarters of the Knights Templar was on the Temple Mount in Jerusalem. In 1139 Pope Innocent II's papal bull Omne Datum Optimum approved Templar's rule and exempted the Order from obedience to local laws, taxes and tithes. This meant that the Templars could move without any limitations through borders, did not have to pay taxes, and were exempt from all any authority except that of the pope. They were allowed also to build their own churches and collect taxes on Templar properties annually.

Another MNC worth to mention is British East India Trading Company, created in the 16th century. Queen Elizabeth I gave a Royal Charter to the company on 31 December 1600. Its objective was to extrapolate economic and other activities of British Empire in the Far East, Africa, and the Americas. The company became so successful and effective that later it processed half of the world's trade, particularly in basic commodities including cotton, silk, tea, and so on. The company also helped to expand the British Empire in India. One of the legacies from British East India Trading Company is the development of Earl Grey tea. The company had recurring issues with their financial situation which resulted in the company being ultimately dissolved in 1874.

MNCs, as we know them today, appeared only by the 19th century when the factory system and better transportation possibilities appeared. During the 19th and early 20th centuries MNCs started to emerge in the Western Europe and United States. Those MNCs invested in the Middle East, Asia, Latin America. Between the First and Second World Wars a big push to MNCs was given due to the need in natural resources.

US MNC were dominant in foreign investment activities in the two decades after the Second World War, when MNCs from Europe and Japan began to play ever bigger roles. Starting 1950s, banks from Europe and United States started to invest large amounts of funds in industrial stocks. This propelled development and mergers of corporations. By 1970 MNCs played an even bigger role due to trends related to air transportation, computers and communications.

During this time, there were around 7,000 MNCs. In the beginning of the 1980s MNCs started to increasingly invest into economies of less economically developed countries. Governments of those countries were interested to attract those investments to get economic growth, create new jobs and get access to technologies. These governments were very interested in attracting MNCs. MNCs are interested in expanding to less economically developed countries because of potential new market for their products and services, and due to lower wages and less strict compliance requirements, which makes doing business in such countries easier and cheaper. Foreign investment in less economically developed countries in 1992 was more than US$50 billion and increased to US$71 billion in 1993 and to US$80 billion in 1994.

Nowadays the number of MNCs is over 41,000.

A lifecycle of a for-profit company, including MNCs, can be demonstrated via such a graphic.

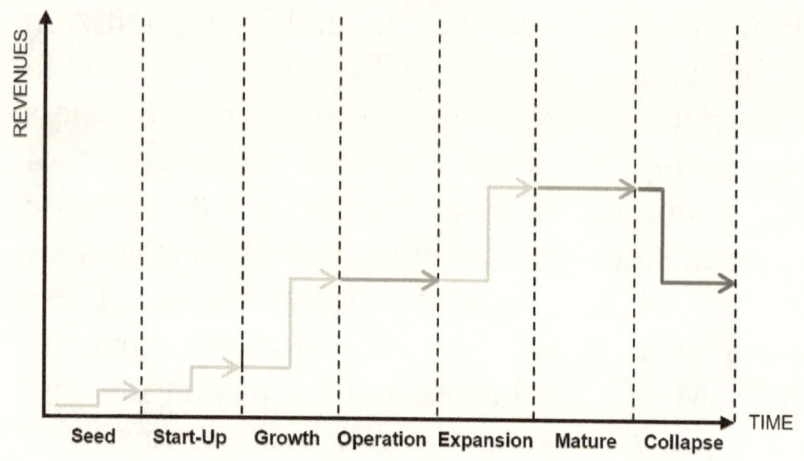

Figure 1. Lifecycle of an MNC

Typically, MNCs have some specifics in comparison to other companies. Let us have a look below what those specifics are, and, to understand them better, try to look at several examples.

1. Increased public and compliance requirements

Majority of MNCs are public companies, e.g. companies whose shares are traded at one or more stock exchanges. The largest stock exchanges are New York Stock Exchange, Nasdaq, Japan Exchange Group, and London Stock Exchange. There are several benefits for MNCs to be listed at stock exchanges. These are:
- Increased access to capital and financing (once the company is public, it has access

to an entirely new, deep and liquid source of capital for any future needs it may have),

- Liquidity event (the initial public offering can be structured such that existing owners of the company can sell down their position and receive proceeds for their shares),
- Branding event and prestige (the company will receive worldwide media coverage through the financial markets), and;
- Public currency for acquisitions (once the company is public, it can use its publicly tradable common stock in whole or in part to acquire other public or private companies in conjunction with, or instead of, raising additional capital).

On the other hand, there are also a few considerations and challenges. One challenge is loss of privacy and flexibility. Public companies must publicly disclose different forms of information (potentially sensitive), which competitors, regulatory agencies, and others will have access to. The second challenge is related to regulatory requirements and potential liability: public companies must regularly file various reports with regulators (for instance, US Securities and Exchange Commission) To be able to be compliant with requirements, companies often need to change the way they document operations and financials, which can be expensive and time-consuming. In addition, directors and officers are potentially liable for potential misstatements and omissions in the registration statement and in the company's ongoing reporting under the Securities Exchange Act of 1934 (the Exchange Act). The Sarbanes-Oxley Act (SOX) was passed in the USA in 2002 as a reaction to several major corporate and accounting scandals, which had cost investors billions of dollars and shook public confidence in the nation's securities markets. SOX identified new standards on transparency and external reporting for those public companies, whose shares were traded at the New-York Stock Exchange. SOX compliance is a challenging process and consumes time and efforts. Furthermore, planning and executing an IPO is a time-consuming process that can distract management from the company's core business. Additional obligations of a public company after an IPO may also take up significant management time.

An example of a corporation that did IPO is one of the largest global e-commerce companies. Being founded in last 1990s, it went for IPO in

2014, being assessed a triple-digit billion-dollar value.

Following a very successful international roadshow, the IPO exceeded any expectations having raised 25% more than planned.

2. Serving global customers

The key reason of internationalization in many industries is to serve global customers. Corporations need proximity to its customers to be able to serve them more effectively and efficiently. Also, a global client may need similar services to all its subsidiaries on the operating countries. This applies to such industries as public accounting and consulting services, legal services, and so on.

'Big 4" auditors (PwC, Deloitte, Ernst & Young and KPMG) that serve global clients across all continents can serve as good examples.

For example, if a global company is an audit client of a "Big 4" company, then offices of that "Big 4" company in the same countries where the client has branch offices apply a similar approach to audit to ensure consistent audit of a global company. If a client requires consulting services, then "Big 4" company office in the country where the headquarters of the client is located can develop a methodology, deploy it to relevant

"Big 4" company offices. "Big 4" company offices will conduct the field work and report the results back to the "hosting" office, where results are consolidated, analyzed, and the project deliverables are submitted to the client's headquarters.

Going further, because of serving global customers and having accumulated global expertise in certain industries, "Big 4" companies have created global industry-specific centers of expertise to provide second level support to local officers and customers.

3. Labor arbitrage

MNCs can leverage efficiencies from locating different activities in different countries (e.g. transactional activities in low-cost countries).

Per International Labor Comparisons from the US Bureau of Labor Statistics, there are very different average hourly compensation costs for different countries and locations. Below is an example for the manufacturing industry.

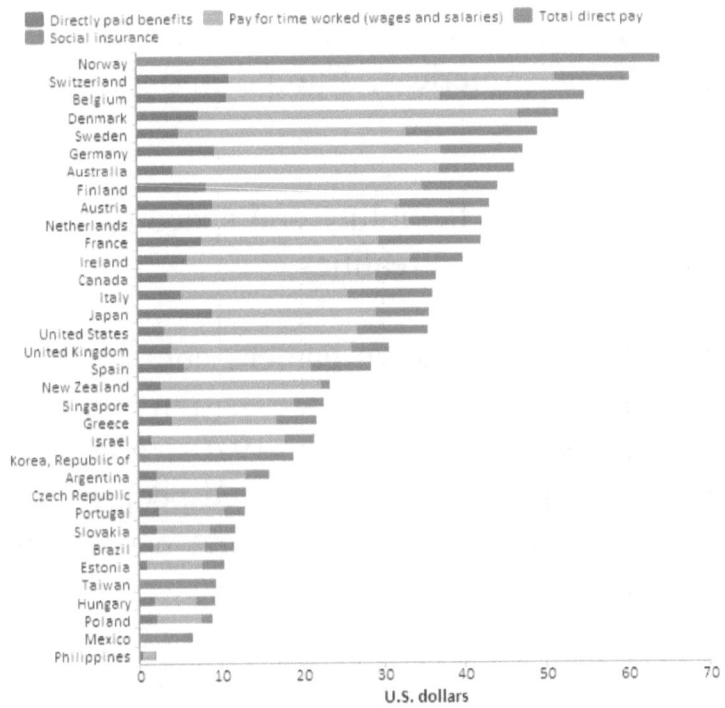

Manufacturing average hourly compensation costs in U.S. dollars, by components of compensation, 2011

Directly paid benefits Pay for time worked (wages and salaries) Total direct pay
Social insurance

Note: For Mexico, Republic of Korea, Norway, and Taiwan, pay for time worked and directly paid benefits are combined into total direct pay.

Source: U.S. Bureau of Labor Statistics, International Labor Comparisons.

Figure 2. Manufacturing average hourly rates

Given such different compensation rates between countries, MNCs would naturally move transactional activities from high cost countries to lower cost countries. Many MNCs created so called "shared service centers" in different locations where they bundled different transactional activities (i.e. call centers, accounting, order processing, contracting, and so on). If MNC works throughout the globe, then such shared service centers can be created in different regions to serve subsidiaries, for example in Americas, Europe and Africa, and Asia.

4. Need in greater flexibility and speed to adapting to changing market realities

One of the well-known camera companies used to manage a significant share of film and camera sales in North America in 1970s, and even a phrase including its name entered people lexicon to describe a personal event that needed to be recorded.

That company was one of the first companies to have developed digital cameras, how the product was dropped for fear it would threaten its core business of films and traditional cameras. In the 1990s, the company planned a journey to move to digital technology. However, the new digital strategy was not really implemented. Its core business faced no pressure from competing technologies, and the management could not imagine a world without traditional film. Later, due to lack of digital strategy, the company lost its market share.

The key reason of that failure was that instead of promoting the new technology, the company held back because of the fear that it would hurt its traditional film business, even after digital products were reshaping the market.

5. Thinking globally, acting locally

To manage an MNC, its leadership team needs disciplined governance and standardized processes. However, the world is very diverse: different countries have different legislation, cultures, market, etc. To be able to operate in different countries, an MNC needs to apply its global strategy for each country it operates in.

A typical example is one of the largest fast-food hamburger chains. It serves millions of customers every day in more than 100 countries.

Values and business principles of that company are universal throughout the world. However, its products offerings are more diverse. Quiche, red bean pie, cabbage soup ... Those are actual menu items at its restaurants around the world. For instance, in Dubai (United Arab Emirates) it sells also chicken hamburgers which consists of Halal grilled chicken patties with lettuce, tomatoes, onions and garlic sauce, held together by Arabic bread. Such a product strategy helps to maximize the addressable market of customers in the countries.

3. TRENDS FORCING TO TRANSFORM

There are multiple trends that enforce MNCs to transform nowadays. Those can be divided into external and internal reasons.

From the external perspective, the key trend is digitalization which many people also call a new industrial revolution. Many processes and operations are being moved into some form of digital format, for example digital check-in instead of physical counters at the airports, digital contracting, and so on. Another trend is new and increasing government regulations which MNCs must comply with. For instance, sanctions against certain countries and sectors make MNCs change their approach. Workforce in different regions and countries also shapes MNCs, a tendency to hire more young talents or millennials is increasing.

Internal reasons include inefficiency in organization and processes, which can lead to lost revenues and increased costs, and employee satisfaction which obviously leads to the same impact.

4. ANATOMY OF CHANGE

Instead of giving standard textbook definitions of change and change management, we will try to identify anatomy of change and take it from there. In this book, we have tried to analyze anatomy of change, e.g. what change comes down to. That is important to know to address, manage, and lead change on a completely different level.

Let us approach the problem of analysis of change in a scientific way. Let us assume that an organization is substance. Our diverse World consists of a lot of substances, some of them are met very frequently in many places, and some of them are very rare. Organizations are like substances: some are more local, some regional, some global, and you can see their brands everywhere you go. Substances consist of molecules. Departments of an organization can be regarded as molecules, even though they are not the same as molecules (in scientific research there is always some approximation). Employees in the departments can be regarded as atoms, which molecules consist of.

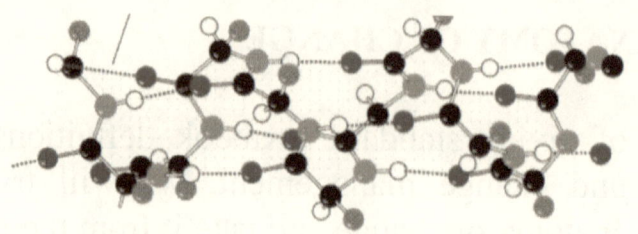

Figure 3. Molecules within substance

In the previous section, we have looked at several trends which make organizations transform. Even though these trends have quite different natures and other attributes, all of them come down to several simple points. If we understand those points, we will be able to effectively manage a change of any nature.

Let us now go bottom-up, e.g. see how any transformation can impact an employee, then a department, and then an organization. To understand what different transformation initiatives, come down to, let us look at three levels: employee, department or organization.

The easiest change is when only work content of an employee changes. For example, an employee is responsible for selling of product A, and now is responsible for product B. Or, for instance, an employee used to be responsible for Customers C, D, and E, and is now responsible for Customers F, and G. This is the easiest change that can happen, and it can be in principle addressed either via content training (either on-the-job training, peer learning, or a dedicated training session). A more difficult change is when an employee must deal with different interfaces that the ones he used to have before to continue to do his task. From the first sight, this change does not seem significant, however it cannot be underestimated. Any new interface creates a potential "bottleneck", an inefficiency, and conflict point due to a personal and cultural difference. There is a low, but still a risk, that the new interface can be ineffective, and with regards to efficiency, it will probably take some time until it becomes as efficient as the interface before. So, this may create a stress and resistance for an employee. To address this, we can consider conducting a workshop, a teambuilding, or a social event. Another level of complexity for an employee is when there is an organizational change of any kind. It can be a new manager, the same manager but reporting to a different department, promotion to a people manager's role, or, in contrary, a change from people manager's role to an individual contributor role. Basically, all such kind of changes is related to the labor contract and labor law of the relevant country. The complexity of this kind of change is because it impacts so called "hygiene" factors for an employee. If a hygiene factor is impacted, it makes no sense to focus on motivation unless the impact is addressed. Depending on the legislation of the country, an approval of an organizational change needs to be secured from relevant social partners, and then it needs to be carefully and diligently communicated to an employee, ideally by the employee's direct manager. There can be situations which consist of a mix of two or three of the above-mentioned changes, and in each of these cases the holistic impact and respective action plan needs to be assessed carefully.

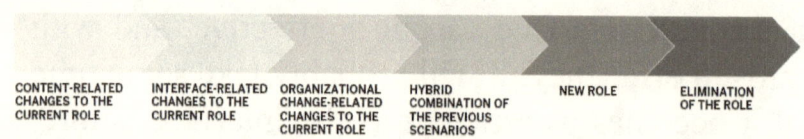

| CONTENT-RELATED CHANGES TO THE CURRENT ROLE | INTERFACE-RELATED CHANGES TO THE CURRENT ROLE | ORGANIZATIONAL CHANGE-RELATED CHANGES TO THE CURRENT ROLE | HYBRID COMBINATION OF THE PREVIOUS SCENARIOS | NEW ROLE | ELIMINATION OF THE ROLE |

Figure 4. Level of impact of different changes on an employee

Another major change is when an employee gets a completely new role. That is usually a positive development for an employee, and usually happens because of progression or a promotion. To address this, we need to leverage proposed action plan from the items one and two below.

The last and the biggest impact on an employee is when employee's role is going to disappear. That can happen due to multiple reasons, for example, personnel lay-off, redistribution of tasks, etc. In such cases, on one hand we need to make sure that an employee is timely and duly notified (including a redundancy package), and on the other hand, if an employee is a talent, then we in parallel need to do our best to find an alternative job for that employee. How to do so is described in the chapter 5.8.

If we now look at a department, basically, all changes impacting a department will come down to the same or similar topics, e.g. department must manage different activities, will collaborate with different departments, will be organizationally reporting to another manager, or will disappear. Impact and action plan for a department is like those for an employee.

REDISTRIBUTION OF   NEW PRODUCT   NEW STRATEGIC
TASKS AMONG   OR SERVICE   PRIORITIES
DEPARTMENTS

Figure 5. Level of impact of different changes on a department

Now the top level – organization by itself. The first result of a change is a change in company's strategy, or strategic priorities. It may wish to make a mid-term or a long-term plan, focus on different objectives or KPIs. Usually, this happens due to an external factor when market share is reducing, or a new technology becomes available, or a new revenue opportunity pops us.

Because of change, an organization may have a new product or service, get rid of or downgrade an old product or service. This is a dramatic change, as it directly impacts the way of doing business, not to mention revenues and costs. Another change can be the result of the previous one – a change in products or services. An organization can introduce or cancel a product or a service. This one is quite significant as well, as it is directly related to revenues and costs. A less critical activity is re-distribution of tasks among organizations' departments or units. This means a change for each impacted unit, as discussed above, and for organization's leadership team this may mean different subordinated, who will be responsible for tasks.

All the changes mentioned above involve employees, directly or indirectly. Normally, by default, employees have resistance to change and transform. Most people are risk averse by nature, because change means to give up habits and this also creates uncertainty about the future.

Therefore, mostly all types of changes initially turn into resistances against those changes. However, as most of projects and initiatives include changes, most of them cause resistance from employees.

Hultman (1995) defines resistance as "a state of mind reflecting unwillingness or unreceptiveness to change in the ways people think and behave." Huczynski (2013) defines resistance to change "as the unwillingness or inability to accept or to discuss changes that are perceived to be damaging or threatening to the individual". Other pole is readiness for change, which means that an individual is ready to welcome and embrace change. Every change has positive and negative aspects. Also, change includes an opportunity to experiment and create something new, however something familiar may be discontinued and stopped.

Thus, resistance to change is natural. There are many reasons for the resistance to change, below are some of them:

- Self-interest
  Employees want to maintain a status quo with which they are familiar and comfortable with. Change will push them outside of their comfort zone, including new tasks or way of working, new relationships or interfaces, etc.

- Lack of understanding
  Employees will resist change if they do not understand the storyline, reasons, and root causes of change.

- Different opinion
  Even if employees understand the reasons for change, they may simply disagree and have a different opinion. However, this can be used to enrich the change storyline based on alternative opinions and make it even better.

- Tolerance towards change in the culture
  Societies differ in their abilities to cope with change and uncertainty. Some people have low tolerance for ambiguity and uncertainty, whereas in other cultures they are more risk averse.

- Appreciation
  Employees may feel that their thoughts, actions, and feelings are not properly valued during change.

- Autonomy
  During change, when certain activities are asked to be done, employees may feel that they are losing freedom of actions and decisions.

- Status in the organization
  Because of reorganization, roles and hierarchies may change, and people may perceive that their roles, during and after change will become less important and lower level.

- Role itself
  Because of the change, if content of roles change, employees may be dissatisfied with the new content of their role.

5. WHY IS CHANGE MANAGEMENT NEEDED?

All the changes described above lead to the fact that during and after transformation the employees and departments become less effective and efficient due to impact on them. The key of change management is to make sure that transformation does not have any negative impact on employees and departments, and on organizations as well, so that the organizations are able to enjoy lasting benefits expected from the transformation.

Why is it so important? Because a change started with most positive intentions, can be run in a way, that it will may have a negative impact on employee engagement. And if employee engagement is decreasing, then it can impact the productivity of the organization. Let us look at that in more detail. What is employee engagement? One of the typical definitions of an "engaged employee" is an employee who is fully absorbed by, and enthusiastic about their work and so takes positive action to further the organization's reputation and interests. There have been many efforts to concretely define employee engagement. Let us see, what the challenges with regards to those are. Engagement does not equal to satisfaction of employees. It is more than that. A satisfied employee will work normal working hours and not complain but will probably not go the extra mile. There is a gap between satisfaction and engagement. Engagement does not equal to happiness either. An employee may be happy at work with relationships to colleagues, work-life balance, but it does not mean that an employee will work hard to help a company achieve objectives. Basically, employee engagement is related to a soft component: to an emotional commitment that employees have towards strategy and objectives of the organization.

It is very well explained with the following legend: an engaged janitorial employee at NASA, when asked what he was doing, is said to have replied "I'm helping to put a man on the Moon"...

Such an emotional commitment leads to the fact that committed employees work harder and go the extra mile to support company aspirations. This leads to higher quality and quantity of work, higher customer satisfaction, and thus higher profits and profitability.

A very good visualization of the impact on employee engagement during transformation can be shown through a "change curve":

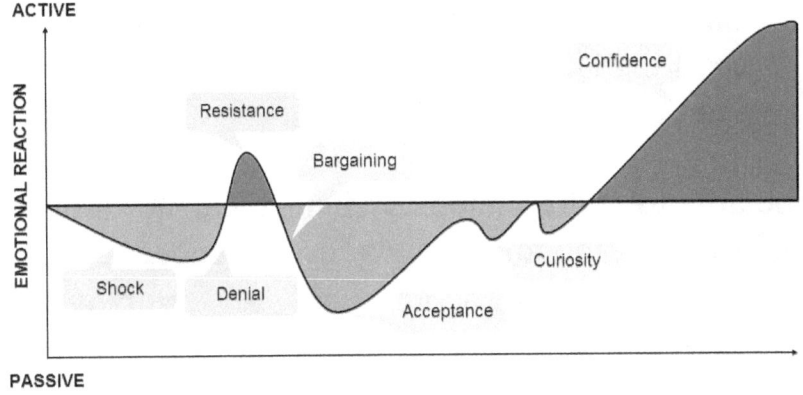

Figure 6. Change curve

Per the report "State of American workforce" by Gallup, Inc.:

- Work units in the top 25% of Gallup's Q12 Client Database have significantly higher productivity, profitability, and customer ratings, less turnover and absenteeism, and fewer safety incidents than those in the bottom 25%.
- Organizations with an average of 9.3 engaged employees for every actively disengaged employee in 2010-2011 experienced 147% higher earnings per share (EPS) compared with their competition in 2011-2012. In contrast, those with an average of 2.6 engaged employees for every actively disengaged employee experienced 2% lower EPS compared with their competition during that same time period.

- Gallup estimates that active disengagement costs the U.S. $450 billion to $550 billion per year.

To be able to address employee engagement during transformation, the following is recommended:
- Conduct and action on an employee engagement survey
- Focus on engagement at all levels of multi-national corporation to reach its furthest corner (from global, to regions, and local)
- Educate managers to be accountable for engagement of their teams and not only manage, but also to inspire and lead the teams
- Take care of employees. Identify, retain, and develop talents.

An effective change management framework addresses all the points above, and thus significantly contributes to company's performance.

To summarize, transformation efforts leading to changes for employees and departments may reduce employee engagement, which may have a negative impact on company performance and negatively compensate expected benefits from engagement. Therefore, proper change management, via addressing the softer component of transformation can ensure that transformation will bring intended lasting benefits to the organization and thus makes sense. Obviously, this works only in conjunction with the hard component, content.

Figure 7. Components of change

6. CHANGE MANAGEMENT IN ACTION

BUILDING A CORE GUIDING TEAM

The first step to prepare transformation is to build a guiding team, who will lead the transformation. Without effective implementation of this step, any further step can be useless.

Having a core leadership team sponsoring and owning the transformation is a crucial success factor. The leadership team needs to be aligned on the objectives and timelines of the transformation. That "tone at the top" will significantly support in driving the transformation. The leadership team should be visible to the employees via different channels (refer to the section 5.9.) and convey the message of alignment on transformation.

What kind of empowerment do the guiding teams need? The core guiding team needs to be aligned on the objectives of the transformation and be one voice on the topic. Therefore, it probably makes sense to conduct a session where members of the guiding team can discuss, align and sign-off on relevant topics:

- Alignment on the strategic context
  - Align on vision for the future
  - Align on the strategic context around the department

- o Align on the strategy for transformation (please, refer to the section on strategy).
  - o Discuss concerns
  - o Discuss expectations and guiding principles

- Understand the work ahead
  - o Align on the extended governance team and work streams
  - o Align on how to manage stakeholders

- Understand own role in transformation process
  - o Leadership roles and support needs have been clarified

If a transformation involves several different areas of the organization, ideally, the leads of those areas should be fully aligned on the transformation objectives and approach.

The key specific for an MNC would be to make sure that the core guiding team is coherent in terms of cross-culture communication as well as including global leads of all transforming departments. It is crucial to have leads of those departments fully aligned on the objectives and other attributes of transformation.

6.2. CREATING SENSE OF URGENCY

Very often change efforts and initiatives fail because of lack of momentum or speed. A sense of urgency can help to change the mindset of employees from the established status quo towards a new state. Without that sense and a resulting change of mindset, it is hard to continue on the transformation roadmap.

A definition of urgency is of "pressing importance" or "pressing necessity." People get a real sense of urgency when they truly believe that action is needed now and not later, when it is convenient. It is about actions which bring results and changes.

True sense of urgency is a positive force, which unites organizations, departments, teams, and people. It helps people to unite efforts and get focused on an objective. Because of that it takes some mental and probably physical efforts for a person to keep the sense of urgency. Naturally people cannot keep that state of mind for a prolonged period, otherwise it there may be a risk of burnout. On the other hand, true sense of urgency is not likely to lead to stress, as it encourages people to focus on and drop less important and relevant activities.

One of the enemies of sense of urgency is complacency. A definition of complacency is "a feeling of quiet pleasure or security, often while unaware of some potential danger, defect, or the like; self-satisfaction or smug satisfaction with an existing situation, condition. ". Several things can lead to complacency. For instance, natural unwillingness of people to change and its consequence on the status quo. That is normal, because people tend to stick to the things that worked in the past, proven things.

A sense of urgency can impact organization's culture. Let us have a look at Schein's model of organizational culture that originated in the 1980s. Schein (2004) identifies three distinct levels in organizational cultures:

- Artifacts and behaviors
- Espoused values
- Assumptions

These layers represent the levels at which organizational culture is seen and experienced by employees:

- Artefacts and behaviors
  At this level, there are the pieces or elements that represent something visible or touchable. For instance, this can be anecdotes at the office, wall posters, the way employees dress, and so on. These are things that are visible and can also be seen and remembered by employees, as well as non-employees (for

instance, an impression that everyone from "Big Four" audit firms wear suit and a tie).

- Espoused values
These values represent the formal values of a company, as well as formal behaviors that need to be adhered to at the company. Quite often, you can find examples of values at this level on formal documents of a company (for example, no compromise on ethics, family first, etc.). These values can be really lived if executives will demonstrate and exercise these values.

- Assumptions
The deepest level, per Schein, is the basic assumptions. These are very deep in minds and of employees, and they exercise those subconsciously. Typically, for someone external to the company, it would be hard to recognize these behaviors.

This framework can be visualized via circles below:

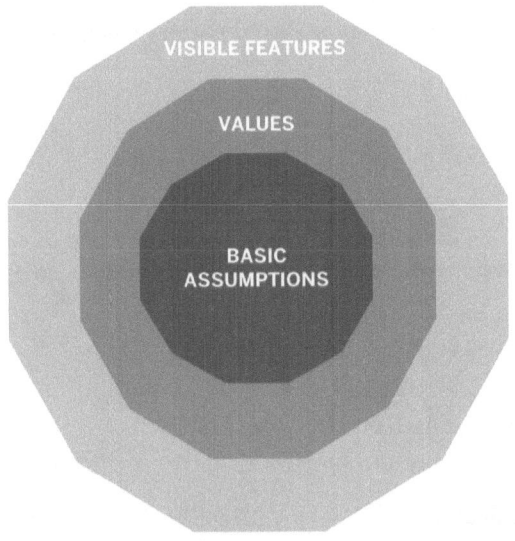

Figure 8. Schein's model of organizational culture

Basically, a sense of urgency can and will likely impact organization's culture, at least for some period. It is very likely to impact and change one or more values, or create additional values, or even to change a basic assumption. Because of that impact, visible features will change.

The best strategy of creating and engaging employees with a sense of urgency, and impact values of organization or even a basic assumption, is to win, not only employee's minds, but also their hearts. In MNCs it is very likely there will be several subcultures with regards to sense of urgency or ultimately transformation.

 Supporters: visionaries, promoters, opportunists

 Sceptics

 Opponents: partisans, candid opponents, emigrants

Figure 9. Subcultures

The supporters will consist of visionaries, promoters, and opportunists.

Visionaries would be of best support of transformation, they would typically have a view on the transformation, would propose new ideas, strategies, and so on. Promoters would buy-in onto the transformation story and would do their best in elaborating the story, rationale, and strategy to their subordinates and peers. Opportunists are those who understand that they can take advantage of transformation to benefit themselves through career or professional development, so their focus on themselves is a priority for them. It is very useful to understand who from employees are visionaries, promoters, or opportunists to get their support in order to drive transformation much more effectively.

Sceptics are those who do not buy in the storyline and even though they will not actively resist or oppose transformation, they will not be ardent supporters.

The last group of employees consists of partisans, candid opponent, and emigrants. Partisans are those who do not support the transformation story and do actions against that, for instance, at meetings they discourage colleagues from supporting the transformation, highlight to colleagues the disadvantages, etc. Candid opponents are those who feel free to publicly disagree with the change. Emigrants are those who, due to disagreement, decide to leave the department or organization. They disagree with the transformation and decide not to work against it but to leave.

A recommendation is to identify the group of supporters and help them as well as to keep an eye on the three last types of employees to make sure that their activities do not do much harm to the transformation.

Let us now have a look at how to create a sense of urgency.

The first method is to "walk the talk". That is to show a tone at the top. The executive leadership team should start to behave with a sense of urgency on a daily basis. Leaders are normally role models in the organization, so their behavior is extremely important. Executive leadership teams and managers are role models for employees, exhibiting the desired behaviors workers should follow. Leadership team sets the tone and standard, for instance, by arriving on time or early, not taking long coffee or lunch breaks, not leaving early unless for urgent business or private reasons. Leadership teams can transmit the sense of urgency through quickly responding to emails, phone calls, and meeting requests. Offices or assistants of the leadership team members in this case play a crucial role in helping leaders to be responsive towards employees. The tone in the organization is set by these leaders: they are in the best position to motivate all employees to work harder, simpler, or be more loyal to the organization.

The second method is to be consistent on communication. At the employee meetings, newsletters, the company leadership should connect the sense of urgency with stories that will be easy for employees to connect with and follow. One of the ways of such communication is to engage employees in transmitting the message of urgency. For instance, you can form group projects to inspire employees by accountability and working on an important subject. To enable all participants to contribute their best, you can assign tasks and duties in that project work based on employee skills and desires. This will help a project to move fast and bring tangible results and can also showcase a new way of collaboration and working.

The third method is to show to employees' content related to the sense of urgency. That can be an external study, internal study, market analysis, any objective data that indicates that a change is needed for an organization. For instance, when an organization set a target to grow its market value, it can choose market capitalization as a key indicator. To show valid justification to employees, an organization can prepare a report showing what the situation is with the current or projected market capitalization of the organization versus those of its main competitors or industry peers.

You may wish to consider using audience-focused communication to share the storyline with relevant employees. Examples may be video clips, interviews, wall posters, and other media (for example, comic strips, cartoons, etc.)

To help create the sense of urgency within an MNC, there needs to be a solid research behind justifying the direction of movement and transformation. The storyline needs to be simple and convincing, so that employees from different continents will buy into the story easily. If you use an audience-focused creative communication, you need to make sure that the content is understood by most employees.

 When we were preparing the first comic for a global corporation to introduce the new program, the idea was to make an analogy between our department and some activity which is fairly popular and most of our employees would know it well. We made a research on what sports were the most popular in the world (i.e. has the maximum number of fans). The following list was created following an analysis:

- Football (soccer)
- Cricket
- Tennis…
- American football
- ..

We decided to go one step further – beyond sports and started to search what topics can most employees connect to. To do so, we started a research on what topics do most people relate to. The results showed that our choice of sports and football was a good fit.

6.3. DEFINING THE SUCCESS AND ESTABLISHING STRETCH TARGETS

It is very important to work on the definition of success. That is needed for all participants of the transformation, for the entire transforming department, or even for the whole organization. Definition of success should be communicated to all involved parties as soon as possible. Everyone should keep it in front of their eyes during the transformation process. This will help ensuring that all efforts, energy, and actions are aimed at reaching the defined success. The definition should be forward-looking, that is, depending on the timelines of transformation, aimed at the time point in the future, when transformation brings already some visible benefits, but not yet be fully completed. To do so, you can use the following wording: "In one year from now…", "In six months from now…", etc. Let us have a look at an example of how to define the success. The definition can be done in a form of a several statements. The first statement can be used to describe the content of transformation. For example, if you transform the sales function, it can be: "we will overachieve the sales volume for first two quarters of the next year…". Another sentence can be used to describe relationships with customers of the department, external or internal.

For example, "We will increase internal customer satisfaction by 12 points". Another sentence can be focused on employees of the transforming department. For example: "We will increase employee engagement by 10 points". You can add additional success definitions, if needed, and depending on the content and scope of your transformation.

In general, all definitions used, represent objectives, or targets. To motivate employees to deliver on those targets, on top of their daily activities, you can consider putting targets, which are challenging, but achievable, i.e. stretch targets. If a target will be too easy to achieve, it may not motivate employees. And in the contrary, if the carrot will be too far from the rabbit, employees may lose motivation and not recognize targets seriously.

It is a good practice to set the targets using the SMART criteria. SMART is used in creation of targets in multiple areas, for instance, in performance management of employees, project management, and so on. For the first time the use of the SMART term happened occurs in Per George T. Doran, every relevant objective should be:

- Specific
  This means that to succeed, one needs a specific goal versus a general goal. The goal must be clear and unambiguous. To make goals specific, one must understand what

exactly is expected, why that goal needs to be set up, who should be involved in setting up the goal, and so on.

A goal can be considered as specific if, the below questions can be answered:

o What: What does the goal help me to accomplish?
o Why: Why am I encouraged to achieve the goal?
o Who: Who is involved in the goal achievement process?
o Where: Where should I put the efforts to achieve the goal?
o Which: Which requirements and conditions must I consider setting up and achieve the goal?

- Measurable
  This attribute is related to the measurement of the goal. It is hard to control anything if it is not measured. Moreover, it is it is impossible to touch base on weather or not a person, tam, department, or organization makes progress if it is impossible to measure that. A goal can be considered as measurable if, the below questions can be answered:
  o How many or how much?
  o How do we know that it is accomplished?
  o How can we quantify?

- Achievable

  This means that a goal must be realistic to achieve, so that it ca be considered as a proper goal. It is ok to have a goal which can lead a person, team, department, or organization to stretch, this even encourages for better results, however If a goal is not achievable at all, it is not a proper one, as such a goal does not motivate.

Figure 10. Carrot always too far from the rabbit

It is not unusual that a stretch goal encourages the goal-setter to find previously overlooked chances and opportunities. A goal can be considered as achievable if, the below questions can be answered:

- How can the goal be achieved?
- IS the goal realistic?

- Relevant
  This means that the goal must be relevant for the strategy. A goal can me specific measurable, achievable, but not relevant. If a goal is not relevant, then the team or department will not buy in, and the goal will not make a difference for the strategy. A goal can be considered as relevant if, the below questions can be answered:
  - Does this contribute to the strategy?
  - Is this the duly time to focus on the goal?
  - Is it applicable in the current macroeconomic circumstances?

- Time-related
  Another important area of goal-setting is that a goal must be achieved and focused on during the proper time horizon. For instance, if a person, team, or a department is committed to a deadline, that helps to focus

and do the best. This attribute helps to establish a sense of urgency, A time-bound goal is intended to establish a sense of urgency. A goal can be considered as relevant if, the below questions can be answered:

- When?
- How much time?

6.4.   STRATEGY DURING THE CHANGE

Another step to start the transformation process is a strategy. A strategy is needed during the change process to keep in mind where the change is heading to and help people to visualize that. It will encourage employees during the change process and help them to feel part of a big story and understand how their actions help the organization or department in transforming. If there is already a strategy, you may re-define it, if there is none, you may create one.

Having a clear strategy gives the following benefits:

- Clear direction

  A strategy will help realize where the organization is currently, where it is going to be and what is needed to take it from here to there. This clarity is much needed, so that employees can align their activities with the strategic objectives. With a proper strategic direction, it is easier to make the transformation be a success.

- Employee engagement
Having a strategy and clear direction will enable employees to dot their best because it will show a direction where their effort should be applied to.

- Analysis of current business
Development of a strategy means a thorough analysis of the current situation of the organization is done. It will help the leadership team to understand better the current business issues via a deep analysis of what is going on, which issues it faces and this helps to better manage the business.

- Future proofing the organization
Creation of a strategy also means that leadership teams are thinking about the future, trends, competition, market share, and what a company needs to do to future proof itself.

Here are some principles which you can use to build your strategy, to be used during the change process. Typically, a strategy has objectives, then priorities aligned with those objectives, and then a foundation or basic principles or presuppositions. Let us look at each of those three elements.

There are many fundamental books and sources on how to create a strategy, which you can consider. Let us look below at a sample process to make a strategy for transformation.

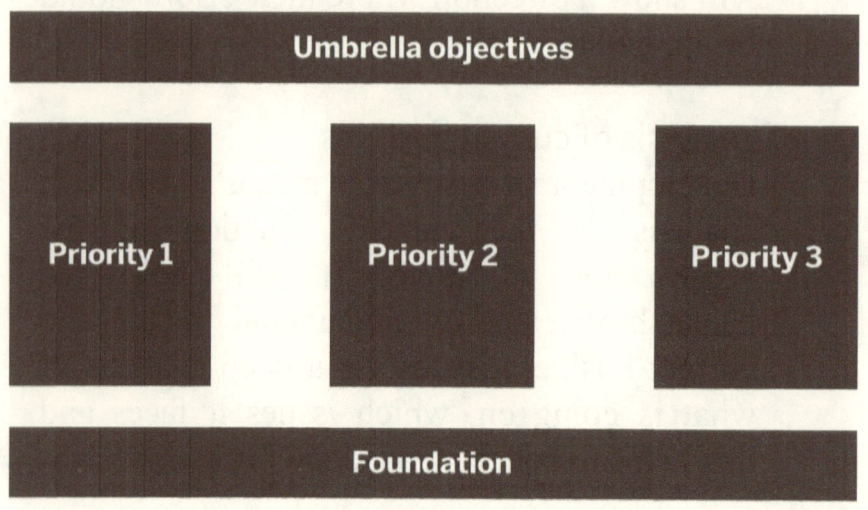

Figure 11. Strategy template

Umbrella objectives

To identify umbrella objectives of your strategy, you need to make an analysis of the entire strategic context around your department.

The strategic context typically includes objectives of the entire organization. Typically, each organization has a mid or a long-term objective. Naturally all the departments of the organization should ultimately work towards achievement of those objectives; therefore, the organization's objectives are part of your strategic context.

Objectives of your external or internal customers

Objectives should be aligned with those of your external or internal customers. If you are transforming a front-office department (e.g. sales, marketing, etc.), then your objectives should be aligned with those of your customers, who buy products or services from you. If you are transforming a back-office department (e.g. finance, human resources, etc.), then your objectives should be aligned with those of your internal customers, e.g. for human resource department, they are all departments that are supported by it, for finance department they are the sales department, etc.

Figure 12. Customer centricity

Customer orientation is crucial for the success of any business. Therefore, on top of having objectives of your customers, you may wish to get more detailed feedback from your customers. That feedback will help you to get an independent view on how you operate and what value you bring. It will also support you in becoming more effective and efficient. Some of the channels to get additional feedback from your customers include:

- Interviewing
  If you interview your customers, consider choosing a representative group. That means to talk to not only executives, but also to normal employees who do the day-to-day job. This will give you a holistic picture on processes on all levels.

- Survey
  In large organizations, a survey may be more relevant due to high number of employees.

There are multiple other ways of getting feedback from internal customers.

Employee satisfaction

Employees are the key asset of each organization. Nowadays many organizations have realized that, and thus employees are becoming more and more visible and recognized.
Many companies perform employee satisfaction surveys on an annual basis, publish results internally and discuss with employees. If your organization does that, you may wish to consider including this as part of objectives of your strategy.

 SAP's 2016 Integrated Report states that a change by one percentage point of the employee engagement index would have an impact of €45 million to €55 million on SAP's operating profit.

Strategic priorities or pillars

Depending on the industry you work in, size of organization, and many other factors, you can have different actions under your strategy. It is a good idea to show those actions to your customers and employees in a simple and structured way. Let us see below an example of a structure.

One group of actions can be dedicated to support of your internal or external customers. We can call it "Customer". This group may naturally include those actions which help you to be closer to your customers, understand and serve them better, exceed their expectations.

Another group could be dedicated to the way your department works internally, e.g. your internal processes, IT systems, efficiency, etc. We can call it "Efficiency". This group may naturally include the following areas of actions which help you to improve the way you deliver your services to your customers, reduction of cost of your services, thus becoming internally more efficient.

And the third group could be dedicated to your organization and people. We can call it "People". This group may include the following actions:

- Demonstration of leadership
- Identification and development of future leaders
- Identification, appreciation, and development of high performers
- Creation of a working environment where employees are encouraged to high perform

Large organizations already usually have processes that address the first three bullet points. Let us have a deeper look at creating a high-performance encouraging environment.

Good examples of activities to create a high-performance culture are recognition programs, both team and individual.

Figure 13. Importance of recognition

In an individual recognition program, creating fair rules is of importance. Those rules should be based on demonstration of values that are encouraged at your organization and exceeding of expectations. Ideally everyone at your organization should be able to nominate an employee for this recognition. Especially important is to properly communicate the recognition program to internal or external customers, so that they can nominate employees deserving recognition. Another aspect to consider is that your department may include subdivisions which may not support your internal or external customers directly or whose job may be focused on transactional tasks in which it is hard to demonstrate overachievement or leadership. In those cases, you may wish to nominate them for operational excellence demonstrated in processing transactional activities.

The nominated and approved winners should be made visible to your entire department at the meeting of all employees, newsletters, and other channels and media that you use. The visibility should include reasoning of nomination, so that all employees observe that company values and high performance are encouraged.

Team recognition is another good tool to encourage high performance. You can create a friendly competition which will help teams to work closer to the same objective. A simple and understandable set up of objectives or KPIs should be defined and tracked on a regular basis. The KPIs should be fair for all participating subdivisions, so that each can achieve it. It is very important to get buy-in from all participation sub-divisions on the KPIs, so that those are fully accepted and not challenged later.

Your strategy should be based on a strong foundation. One of the ideas could be to consider values or initiatives that are across your entire organization. Such a foundation will be aligned with the entire organization and will represent a solid basis that will go across all the actions in your strategy.

 Tesla's mission is stated as to "accelerate the advent of sustainable transport by bringing compelling mass market electric cars to market as soon as possible".
Facebook's mission was changed "to bring the world closer together ". Unilever's mission statement is "to make sustainable living commonplace".

Implementation

Once the strategy is created, it should be discussed and aligned among the leadership team. Everyone should understand and support it, to make it successful. The strategy will include several action items, and a good idea is to give ownership of those action items to the members of the leadership team.

Figure 14. Example of strategic priorities

This will enable executive sponsorship of action items and empowerment of teams, who will work on implementation of those actions. Progress of all action items should be tracked regularly, and the leadership should also on a regular basis review overall progress.

To implement the strategy in the organization, you need first to communicate it. These are the main ways to communicate:

- Presentation by the leadership team at the meeting of all employees
- Newsletters/emails to all employees
- Posters and flyers outlining the key aspects of the strategy
- Discussion groups (physical and virtual)

- Strategy ambassadors to help convey the messages

A mix of these channels should be continuously used to interact with employees. Below are some further ideas to be considered during implementation of the strategy:

Over time you may observe that some actions may not be implemented in the way you have planned or not implemented at all. This is normal and natural. It can turn out that one or more of the identified actions have not proven themselves as strategic priorities. The best way to handle that is to remove that action from the strategy and reallocate assigned resources to another more important mission.

You also need to constantly monitor the strategic context around your organization or department to update the umbrella objectives, priorities, and the foundation of your strategy when needed.

6.5. BUILDING AN EXTENDED GUIDING TEAM

Now let us see how we build and align an extended leadership team. The mission of such a team is to support the core guiding team and local/country leaders in implementing the transformation. Let us call them "transformation managers".

Quite a comprehensive list of activities of a transformation manager looks as follows:

- Partner with the management team (of a department or organization undergoing through transformation) and promote the transformation program and co-drive related changes
- Own relevant change management and communication plans and oversee execution of those
- Serve as a single point of contact for questions from employees of the department or organization undergoing through transformation
- Understand the impact of the transformation program onto the department or organization and provide that feedback to the project leadership team
- Support the management team in creating individual action plan for impacted employees

- Collaborate regularly with peers from other departments or organizations to exchange best practices
- Assist the management team in organizing workshops and staff meetings related to transformation
- Help the management team to develop and deliver materials on the impact of the transformation to internal or external customers
- Interact with Human resourced department on action plans for impacted employees and collaboration with relevant social partners

A network of transformation managers is by itself a framework. And below you will find an example of how it looks like.

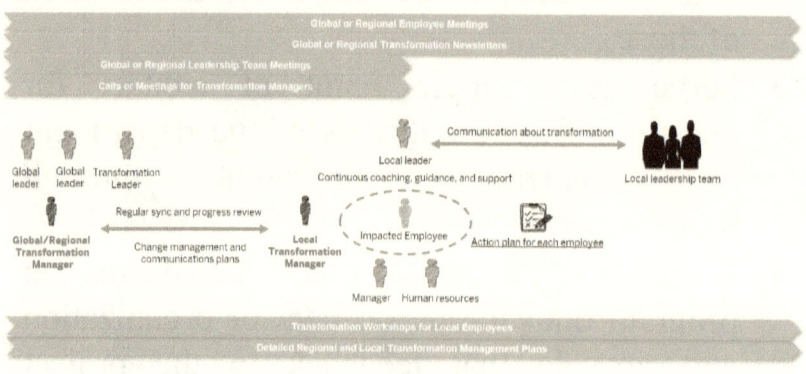

Figure 15. Transformation managers' framework

To make sure that the framework operates, it is a good idea to have someone overseeing it from the regional or global level, depending on the structure of your company and specifics of your transformation project.

Empowerment is needed depending on the objectives and mission of the team. Based on tasks of transformation managers outlines above, the following empowerment would make sense for Transformation managers:

- Feeling of empowerment and mandate from the guiding team

  One of the features of working in a MNC is that probably some of the colleagues who must work with are in different countries and even continents. A person may report to a manager residing in a different country; however, he or she has stakeholders in the local office. Those stakeholders may belong to other departments and be higher in the hierarchical structure. For a transformation manager to be able to effectively support employees, he or she needs to have a clear mandate and empowerment from the core guiding team. Mandate is best to be fixed in the form of a communication, and empowerment – in the form of an interaction with the core guiding team. The core team can have a kick-off meeting or a call with transformation managers to communicate the mandate and give directions, guidance, and expectations. This will enable transformation managers to feel as part of the team.

- Soft skills to engage impacted employees to communicate transformation
  To enable soft-skills component of transformation for transformation managers, the following topics can be considered for their empowerment: preparation for leading the transformation, understanding the transformation storyline, impact on employees, potential reaction of employees to the transformation, communication to impacted employees, understanding how to transmit the transformation storyline and related impacts to the impacted employees, managing reaction of impacted employees, and knowing how to address anxiety, resistance, emotions and other reactions of impacted employees.

It is better to conduct these trainings and empowerment activities as soon as the transformation managers are appointed and when the transformation project is announced to the impacted department.

These trainings can be done within 1 month in small sessions, so that people are not distracted from their daily tasks, and still have an opportunity to upskill.

Representatives of the extended guiding team will need to work closely with the country heads of their departments as well as Human resources department, if there is an impact on employees. Human resources colleagues will help the transformation process, typically with the following tasks:

- They work jointly with Manager and Transformation Manager in change processes;
- Offering sparring / exchange with Manager, Transformation Manager and Recruiting on potential job offerings for affected employees;
- Supporting employees in sensitive situations;
- Driving execution of HR relevant topics within the change/transformation process;
- Driving and managing business organizational development;
- Informing the managers and Transformation Managers about the outcome of consultations with social partners (respecting the confidentiality guidelines) and breaks down the information to the individual case of the affected employee;
- Leveraging the HR Network and supporting the process between sending and receiving business unit in a transfer process;

- Supporting manager and employee in defining individual development/action plan if necessary:
- Informing about available trainings and programs.

6.6. MANAGING CUSTOMERS AND STAKEHOLDERS

One of the secrets of success is to serve the customers well. Customer centricity is key and is in the heart of any business. Therefore, it is crucially important to keep your customers (external or internal) well managed and informed during the transformation process. Let us see below one of the useful tools for that purpose – stakeholder impact analysis.

Stakeholder Analysis is a method to figure out the key people who should be won over. The results of the exercise can help understand how to manage stakeholders during the transformation.

Customer/stakeholder-based approach brings the following benefits:

- Most powerful stakeholders or customers will provide an expert opinion which can be used at an early stage of the transformation. This will most likely increase the overall quality of transformation as well as gain engagement of stakeholders

- Support from a stakeholder may help to get more resources which helps the transformation, and it increases the likelihood of the successful outcome of transformation
- A stakeholder will better understand the rationale and objectives of the transformation and will thus better support if needed

The table below includes some of the parties who might be stakeholders or customers during the transformation:

Your manager	Company Shareholders	Government authorities
Customers	Alliance partners	Trades associations
Colleagues/peers	Suppliers	Mass media
Employees in your department	Auditors	Social partners

Figure 16. Stakeholders of transformation

Even though stakeholders or customers may be teams, departments, or whole organizations, it is important to note that one must ultimately communicate with people, thus it will be useful to identify the correct individual stakeholders within a stakeholder organization.

A good approach could also be to list the people, teams, and departments who may be impacted by operational tasks of your department and analyze it to identify who has the power to support or block, who is interested in transformation and who does not care at all.

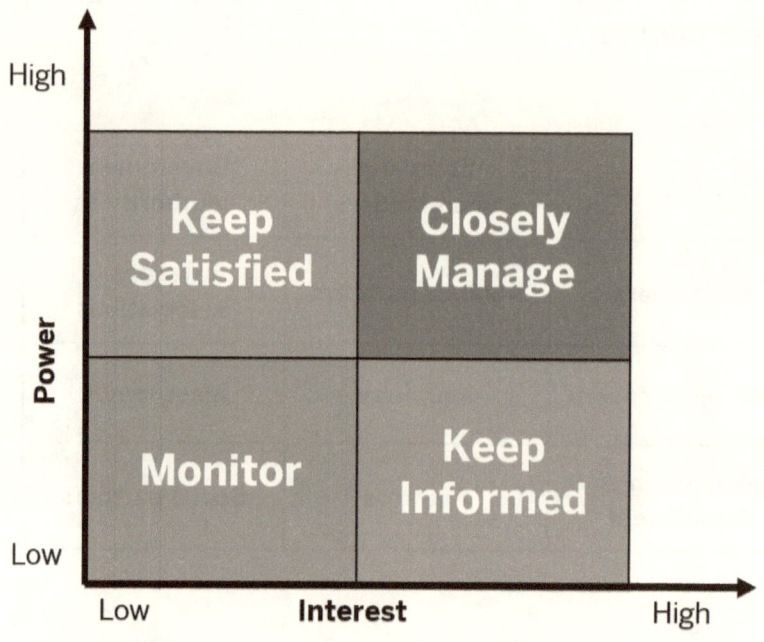

Figure 17. Activities for stakeholder groups

Let us look at an example. For instance, if you lead a regional or local department, an executive head of a global department is very likely to have high power and influence over your projects and high interest in its results and outcome. Your family will likely have high interest but are unlikely to have much power with regards to that.

The position of a stakeholder on the graph shows the proposed activities we must do to optimally address their needs:

- High power, High interest: we should deeply engage with these parties and make the biggest efforts to satisfy.
- High power, Low interest: we should make these parties satisfied, but not over communicate, so that we do not create irritation.
- Low power, High interest: keep the parties appropriately informed, to make sure that there are no issues arising. These parties can be very helpful for the transformation execution.
- Low power, Low interest: monitor these parties but not over communicate and over interact with them.

We need to know as much as possible about our customers and stakeholders. Their attitude and reaction to transformation is of high importance for us. Also, we need to understand how to engage them in the transformation, how to provide them with status updates and other relevant updates. Below are some of the questions that will help us to learn better our customers or stakeholders:

- What is their objective and financial interest?
- What is their emotional stake?
- What are the benefits and threats for them from the transformation?
- What motivates them?
- What information would they need?
- How do they want to receive that information? What channels are the optimal for communication?
- What is their current opinion of performance of our team or department?

A good option of answering some of these questions would be to take this information directly from the customer or stakeholder.

Because of analysis of those questions for your customers and stakeholders, you can out the results on the grid, as reviewed above. Please, refer to an example below. Color coding will help to show supporters in green, critics in red, and others who are neutral in orange, for instance.

6.7. DEVELOPING A NEW ORGANIZATION

The picture of the future state should be very clear. Ideally it should be understood in the very beginning of the transformation to be able to give as cleaner as possible guidance to employees. The approach to rebuild the plane in the flight, of course, can work and be effective, but not sure, how efficient that can be.

As there are different levels of change, as discussed in the chapter 2 (Anatomy of change), let us review the most complex version, e.g. when new organizations with new missions and tasks are created. First, we need to understand what the objectives of the new organization are, what will be its inputs and outputs for the company, including interfaces with other organizations, then we need to be clear on the key performance indicators and how the organization's performance and success will be measured.

After that we understand what the processes in the new organization are, then from processes we need to transition to tasks and roles in the new organization. For each role, we need:

- Detailed list of tasks;
- Interfaces with other roles, within and outside the organization;
- Key performance indicators;

- Matching profile (in terms of soft and technical skills).

After we have understood this, we need to fill in the roles with people. If the organization is taking over some or all tasks from existing or to-be-eliminated organizations, then we need detailed transfer matrices of tasks and people on who will hand over which tasks to whom.

The new/receiving organization should pull knowledge and tasks from the old/sending organization(s), and there should be a joint agreement on the go-live and stabilization period.

An opportunity to build a brand-new organization is a great occasion for building effective and efficient processes driven by employees who are well matching their roles.

One of the good approaches to build a strong new organization is to use the "7 C's framework".

Figure 18. 7 C's framework

The first element to address is clarity. Clarity is about knowing what the new organization wants to accomplish and how to accomplish. Basically, it is about the strategy of the new organization and its processes. That was in detail discussed in chapter 5.4. It is just important to mention that this element aligns employees' actions. The reaction of an employee in the new organization can be one of the following:

- Compliance/support without buy-in;
- Resistance;
- Identification/support with buy-in;
- Internalization.

Compliance and resistance can be ways to respond to formal authority, and identification to internalization – to informal authority.

The second element is team organization and size. The optimal size of the team ultimately depends on the task. For a too small team it will be difficult to deal with the complexity of the task, a too big team it will be difficult to manage. A general recommendation is if a team is successful, to keep it together for as long as period possible. When defining the future organization, department, or a team, the recommended guidance is to consider not only technical skills, but also personality, perspectives, and social skills. The following questions need to be answered for that purpose:

- What technical competences do you need in the organization, department, or a team to successfully deliver on the strategy;
- What level of skills is needed;
- What kind of diversity is needed, e.g. diversity in personalities; diversity in terms of demographics, or other diversity.

This means that ideally team members should be appointed not only based on technical skills, but also based on diversity of personality, social skills, etc.

Figure 19. Diverse teams win

However, diversity is not only an advantage which brings to a collectively broader range of knowledge, expertise, skills, and higher quality of work and ideas. It may also have not positive consequences, e.g. when employees with similar background tend to be attracted to each other, it may also lead to a confrontation or conflict.

The third element is cohesion. There are practices to build cohesion, and they serve their purpose, i.e. are very effective. These practices help to create motivation among team members and make them really committed to the success of the team. That is important when there are stretch targets, duration of work efforts or projects is long, level of stress is high, and it is uncertain what the outcome will be.

The fourth element is motivation or "carrots". It is about incentives, and we need to make sure that there are the right monetary and non-monetary incentives. Money plays the role of a motivator to a certain level only.

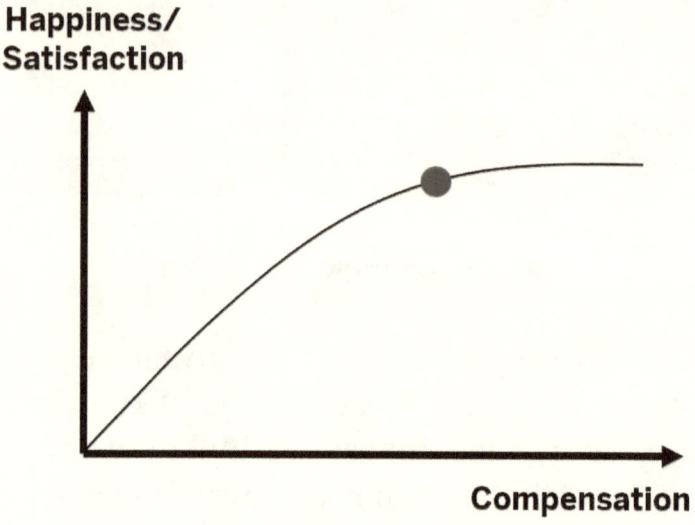

Figure 20. Compensation and satisfaction

Some level of money serves as a hygiene factor, i.e. if not taken care of, that may cause extreme dissatisfaction. However, as the level of satisfaction increases, for each person there is a point, when money does not play anymore the role of motivator. And here other tools need to be used. If a manager needs to motivate employees in a short-term perspective to achieve some fast results, then things like targeted monetary incentives, inspirational conversations and other related things can be used. If the objective is to enable mid- and long-term performance and satisfaction, then a combination of the following measured needs to be used:

- To enable positive emotions, pleasure, and fun – assign the most suitable tasks to an employee, improve the climate at workplace, conduct special events; and
- To highlight the importance of work done by an employee – apply different leadership techniques and show a future vision and the role of employee and his/her work in delivering on that vision and align objectives of an employee with bigger objectives of a team, department, or organization.

The next element is cooperation or competition among team members. On one hand, we have a cooperation, and on the other hand we have a friendly competition, and both option serve the purpose of maximize performance of team, department, or organization. On the friendly competition piece, please refer to chapter 5.4.
Another element is communication.

Figure 21. Flaws in communication

Other employees have influence on performance of an individual. In case a task is easy, an impacted individual is likely to provide the right answer or solution, i.e. impact is positive. In case a task is difficult, an impacted individual is likely to provide the incorrect answer. This means that not all teamwork should be done in teams, and there are some tasks which are better to do individually (e.g. generation of ideas, solving problems, etc.).

In team work, when communication breaks, people tend to blame others. This is because people typically believe that is communication fails, it is due to the other party. Most people tend to rate themselves as having better communication skills than they do.

When there is a communication among a group to decide, it can lead to some unexpected conclusions.

For instance, there may be an illusion of invulnerability, which means that the group may feel that it is collectively wise and can make only a right decision. If there is a view which is opposite from what a group thinks, it is viewed from a simplistic or stereotyped manner. People who are self-conscious may decide to not voice points of view which are contrary to the group's point of view. Because of this, a decision made by a group may be with much lower quality than the one made by an individual. What can be done to prevent such a suboptimal process from taking place? The following recommendations may be helpful:

- Mention and emphasize strategic objectives;
- Establish a free flow of information and data among group members;
- Try to look for anonymous opinions;
- Try to combine ideas of several group members;
- Have a "devil's advocate" in the group.

The last, but not least element is conflict which needs to be managed. It is about incompatible opinions, interests, values, principles, behaviors, and so on. Obviously, in most cases conflict is a negative thing, however ion some cases it can be positive. It can help to come to better ideas and may encourage creativity and innovation. To manage a conflict, it is useful to try to identify its core, e.g. is it related to tasks, relationships, values. A recommendation on how to deal with conflicts can be a general one or specific ones. General recommendations include practicing visionary leadership to highlight the strategic priorities and use personal power. Specific recommendations include:

- Exchanging opinions and views in case of a task conflict;
- Improve communications and re-evaluate interdependencies in case of a relationship conflict;
- Change interdependencies in case of a value conflict;
- Ensure fairness of procedures and policies in case of a conflict related to resources.

6.8.   MANAGING IMPACT ON EMPLOYEES

One of the assumptions used in this book is that employee engagement significantly impacts organization's financial result, and thus must be maintained. Transformation may and will impact employee engagement, and thus we need to make sure that employee engagement is taken care of during transformation.

One of the ideas that this book proposes on change management and employee engagement is to turn quantity into quality. It is very hard to determine the exact amount of anxiety and frustration that an employee or group of employees can have during a transformation, thus the approach proposed in this book is to do as much as possible in terms of quantity until the actions done together will have a major effect in terms of quality.

Let us remember the change curve, described in the chapter 2. The curve gives us an understanding of the stages of perception of change by employees. Let us see below some ideas on how to support employees at different stages of the journey through the curve.

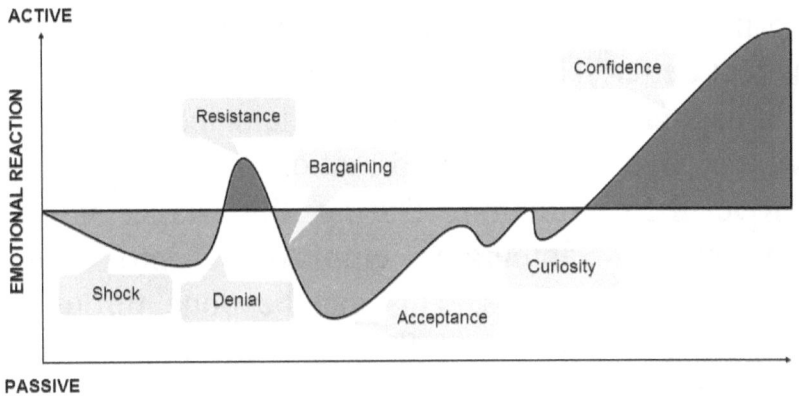

Figure 22. Change curve

Stage "Shock". In this stage people are overwhelmed with information about the changes that will impact them and feel shocked. Here the optimal actions to be conducted by leaders of transformation or managers would be to explain what is going on. Why the transformation was started and what is the objective. It is useful to have a platform to raise questions and get answers. Stage "Denial" starts when employees want to protect and remove themselves from the change. Prior to this stage, an extended guiding team should be established to elaborate to employees the storyline of change, help identify what this means for employees. The next step, called "Anger", is a result of evolution of the previous stage and comes when employees feel negative about the transformation. Here transformation leaders can offer an environment to employees where they can safely raise their concerns, discuss what is going on, and thus feel better. The next step is called "Bargaining" and it happens when employees understand that they have to live with transformation and want to improve their situation. During this stage, it is important to integrate employees into the transformation process. This can be done through involving employees to define how to transform as well as staying firm with message. The next step is called "Grief". It is the lowest point where employee's emotional state can go, and leaders of transformation need to acknowledge the past world and experience, past roles and processes. The next step is "Curiosity". During this step an employee is ready to absorb information of the new organization and is even actively looking for that. To support this step, leaders of transformation can identify and share quick wins about the new organization, identify and discuss the lessons learned, support and train employees. And the best stage here is called "Self-Confidence" when employees feel comfortable with the new organization, have accepted it and live it. Here it is important to celebrate successes, continue to encourage employees and keep an eye on continuous improvement.

Transformation can bring you more efficient processes, lower costs, and other benefits. However, one of the risks associated with transformation is losing key employees. Of course, transformation can be used to depart with those employees with whom the organization does not win-win relationships, but a key success factor is to keep key employees or talents at the organization.

Very often when employees learn about a transformation project which will impact their department, the key question for them is whether they are in or out, i.e. whether they will have a job, or they will not have a job. This leads to the act that employees start losing focus on quality of their work, and this multiplied by key and talented employees leaving can pose a risk and challenge the expected benefits of the transformation.

Therefore, it is important to invest in keeping talents at the organization. Transformation will likely change the scope of tasks of existing employees. To do so, you will need to do several steps. Number one, you need to identify the new roles in the future organization. For that purpose, you need to:

- Identify what is the optimal landscape of new roles;
- Define the new roles (exact scope, skills needed, processes, and performance measurement);
- Understand who from the current organization will move to the new roles;
- Identify for each person, if there is a gap of skills to move to the future role.

Let us talk about each of the above areas. To identify what is the optimal landscape of new roles, you need to think about the objectives that need to be reached. What is the most efficient way of reaching? You can wish to consider 4 types of roles. Type 1 is generalist, who can handle a lot of areas. Type 2 is a trusted advisor, or business partner. You can also call that type a Front office. Type 3 is an expert, who knows well an area and can do provide expert services. Type 4 is a specialist in data entry or processing. You may wish to consider these or also different roles in the landscape of the new organization.

After that, for each new role, it is very useful to make role definition as detailed as possible. The definition should include hard skills needed, definition of process steps owned by that role, input and output information, and key performance indicators for performance measurement and assessment). On top of that the definition should include soft skills required for each role. Examples of four roles described above require quite different soft skills. For instance, type 2 (trusted advisor, or a business partner) needs to be with great communication and persuasion skills, should be able to work fast and make quick and high-quality summaries of large portions of information. Type 3 (an expert) needs to be a person who knows an expert area topic very well and can provide expertise advisory to offices in different regions, or different countries in the same region, should not be in rush and should be able to make thorough expert conclusions or recommendations. To summarize this, the more detailed is any future role defined, the better. One important aspect to consider in identification of the future landscape and in definition of future roles is a perspective. To make the new organization attractive for talents, it is better to show to employees a career path for each role.

The next step after detailed definition of new roles is identification of which existing employees will likely to move to new roles. There can be different ways of doing so depending on local labor legislation of the countries in scope. If an existing employee is a 'natural fit' to the new role, then it can be possible to transfer that employee, depending on the local legislation. But the best way is to pose the new vacancies and invite all interested employees to apply, to make sure that the process is transparent and fair, and employees with skills best matching the role roles will be selected.

There may be employees who may refuse to move to the new organization due to different reasons. One of the reasons can be narrowing of tasks, or lack of career path in the new world.

 Per Adam Smith's Wealth of Nations book, "the greatest improvement in the productive powers of labor… seem to have been the effects of the division of labor".

On the other hand, per Karl Marx's Economic and Philosophical Manuscripts, increasing the specialization may also lead to workers with poorer overall skills and a lack of enthusiasm for their work. The worker then becomes "depressed spiritually and physically to the condition of a machine".

However, let us have a look at the scenario, when new roles are published for open application. For transparency and fairness reasons when several new roles, created due to transformation, is announced, there needs to be some preparatory work.

All the detailed information on the content of new roles, qualifications needed, key stakeholders, and development path, needs to be shared and discussed with eligible employees well in advance to enable employees to prepare themselves.

There are ways of doing so.

Number one, all available information on the new roles should be stored on a media available to all employees who are eligible to apply. That can be organization's internal portal page, a shared drive, or something else. The media should always be kept updated and accessible.

Number two, country managers within the transforming department or transformation managers should organize local sessions for employees in transforming departments to discuss all available information on new roles. They should also have one-to-one conversations with each employee to assist them in making decisions about where they may be best suited in the future organization. Managers should encourage them to read the information about future roles and teams and think about where they can add the most value for themselves and for the organization.

Number three, in a way of a coordinated effort, hiring managers should present to employees' information about the vacancies they are hiring for. For the sake of transparency, this should be conducted in sessions for all eligible employees. The session is best to start from an introduction of an executive sponsoring the project, to demonstrate executive support, then a short update on the status of the project, hiring guidelines, and then each hiring manager discussing qualifications needed and content for each vacancy. In case of no questions at the end of the call, will be good to make a recording of the session and send it to employees to review and ask questions later via an email.

For MNC, where one of the global departments is impacted, you may wish to consider conducting either 3 sessions (1 for Americas, 1 for Europe/Africa, and 1 for Asia), 2 sessions (in the morning for Asia and Europe, in the evening for Americas and Europe), or even 1 session (approximately, at 2:00 pm Central Europe Time, which is 08:00 am Eastern Standard Time, 08:00 pm Singaporean time). After the list of employees, who will move to the new organization, is clear, you will need to identify what will it take to transfer an employee from a current disappearing role to a new future role. In the best case an employee already has all the necessary hard and soft skills to expectedly successfully perform at the new role. In other cases, there will be a gap of skills, both hard and soft. The mission will be to identify those gaps for each employee who will transfer and make an action plan to close that gap. One of the options to approach that is to get information from the direct manager of an employee, then from a manager who interviewed that employee, or from to have a meeting or a conversation with employee. Because of that, there will be identified a list of gaps, which needs to be closed. It is recommended to identify gaps for all or majority of employees in the cope to make a targeted action plan and leverage economies of scale, for example one training on soft skills for all employees.

To complete the picture with regards to retention of employees, we need to discuss enablement of employees.

We can categorize those in the following way:

Short-term
Training to apply for internal roles. During work tenure many employees get their CVs outdated, forget how to behave during interviews, etc. This will help them to increase their chances to get the job if a job opportunity exists.

A website InterviewSuccessFomula.com conducted a survey in and analyzed identified facts about job interview process. Let us have a look at 7 interesting findings:

1. There were 3.6 million job openings at the end of 2012. About 80% of available jobs are never advertised.

2. The average number of people who apply for any given job: 118. Twenty-percent of those applicants get an interview.

3. Many companies use talent-management software to screen resumes, weeding out up to 50% of applications before anyone ever looks at a resume or cover letter.

4. On average, interviews last 40 minutes. After that, it usually takes 24 hours to two weeks to hear from the company with their decision.

5. What do employees look for before making an offer? About 36% look for multitasking skills; 31% look for initiative; 21% look for creative thinking; and 12% look for something else in the candidate.

6. In the U.S., 42% of professionals are uncomfortable negotiating salary. By not negotiating, an individual can lose more than $500,000 by the time they reach 60.

7. More than half (56%) of all employers reported that a candidate rejected their job offer in 2012.

Mid-term

For employees to broaden their horizons in general and get a better understanding of the peers and other interfacing teams or departments, you may wish to consider implementing a rotational program among different departments. The program should ideally operate among those teams and departments that interface with each other. An employee from one department can be chosen to spend some time and conduct operational work in another department for some period. Period depends on the needs and exact objectives of the rotational program and can last from 1 or 2 weeks to 6 months and 1 year. During the rotation, employee will establish working and informal relationships with an interfacing department, better understand the objectives and challenges of that department, and broaden his or her horizons in general. The receiving department will also better understand the objectives and agenda of the sending department; thus, such a model is good for gelling working relationships. One should choose participants, scope, and duration of the rotation carefully to meet the objectives of the program. Ideally, there should be an exchange or a swap of employees between and even among the participating departments. A challenge is related to the work of a rotating employee and swapping employees can be one of the ways to address this.

One of the offerings that can be considered valuable is to help employees to build a career plan. In fact, majority of employees in the companies do not have a clear understanding or a plan on their career. Therefore, it is mutually beneficial for an organization and an employee if organization encourages employees to have such a plan, especially in the beginning of the transformation, when it is known that roles of some employees will be impacted or even will disappear.

Long-term
Good personal presentation, digital literacy and presence on business-relevant social media, team working, collaboration and co-operation, timekeeping and personal organization are among criteria of employability. Ideally employees should be encouraged to address all criteria to maximize their employability within and outside organization. Of course, it is not-favorable outcome if a high-performing employee can leave a team for another one or can even leave the company, however it is fair and good to do so.

If transformation leads to redundancy of some roles, it is important to think about a strategy on communication and execution of that. The best way to do so, is an open and timely communication. In case roles of employees from a global department from different countries are disappearing, to prevent any rumors, one can use the so-called "follow the sun" approach. The approach envisages having notification meetings at 09:00 am in each country and start to do so from the most eastern countries and complete with the most western countries. Such an approach will help to prevent rumors and speculations and keep morale of those employees who will stay on board and be part of the future organization.

6.9. MAINTAINING TRUST

Engagement reflects how an employee feels about the company and how he or she approaches work because of those feelings. When an employee is highly engaged, he or she is more likely to use discretionary effort to go above and beyond regular responsibilities to support and drive business results. What's more, engagement has a proven link to productivity, profitability, customer satisfaction, employee retention and more. Considering today's competitive business environment, building employee engagements is key to driving and achieving the high-performance standards necessary for success

When we think of trust and what it means, we quickly realize it encompasses many things. We use the word "trust" to:
- Mean what people say;
- Describe how people behave;
- Understand if we want and feel comfortable to share information, we have with others;
- Understand if we feel other people have the same or similar interests to what we have;

In the context of social interactions, trust means several things. When someone defines, what trust is, a situation characterized by the following is meant: one party wants to count on another party. On top of that, the party who trusts, has some control over the actions conducted by the other party. Because of this, the party who trusts is not sure about the outcome of actions conducted by another party. In such a situation, only expectations can be used to measure that. And there is some level of uncertainty about the outcome which involves the risk of failure if the other party does not do what is expected.

Trust is about relationships between people. Trust is also applicable relationships within and between groups of people (families, friends, communities, organizations, companies, nations etc.). According to the book, "Trusted Advisor", the trust equation composes of the following:

$$\mathbf{TRUST} = \frac{(\text{CREDIBILITY} + \text{RELIABILITY} + \text{INTIMACY})}{\text{SELF-ORIENTATION}}$$

Figure 23. The trust equation

Let us have a look at how to create trust in the context of an organization and one-to-one discussions. In the context of an organization, there are several ways to do so during transformation. Enablement and information to managers

People managers in the department undergoing through transformation play a crucial role in driving transformation. Each time before a wide communication on significant upcoming changes, it is a good idea to provide a heads-up to managers to prepare them. A heads-up can be done through a dedicated call with all managers, an email communication, and other channels. The preferred way is to do so in a physical meeting, but in large organizations with several locations it is not always possible.

- Heads-up and Information packs to employees
  On top of similar communication process, as the one for managers, you may wish to prepare a frequently asked questions document with detailed answers. This document will be a good reference for employees on many questions.

- All-Hands
  All-hands meetings can be conducted physically or virtually. The recommendation is to do it physically, but this may not be the case for MNCs. Then an optimal way is that the presenters get together with employees in those locations where they are, and all are connected via virtual collaboration tools. On top of showing an update on key business

topics, transformation process, it makes sense to ask an executive and an employee to share a personal story. An executive may talk about personal career insights; give advice on growth and development. An employee may talk about an interesting experience on participation at a major project or an initiative. On top of that would be useful to share an update on the winners of individual and team recognition programs (please refer to 5.4).

- Dialogue sessions with executives
Normally employees appreciate a lot meeting with executives. Such meetings demonstrate that executives are interested in employees, value them, and are ready to use their limited time to talk to them, hear their feedback and answer questions. In many cases, such a meeting can already significantly improve employee engagement. Below are some ideas to be considered for preparation of such sessions.
Objective and agenda
Key objective is increase of employee engagement via giving to employees a better understanding of the transformation journey and personal attention from executives. It may make sense to start form summarizing the objectives and key points of the

transformation, then to have an interactive session among executives and employees on the most pressing questions from employees. Executives should be able to provide comprehensive answers to those questions or commit to follow-up.

Participants
Number of participants plays a crucial role in effectiveness of the meeting. It should so allow a healthy dialogue and not an endless discussion. When choosing participants, you should consider making it diverse group consisting of managers and employees from different departments. No more than 2 executives, otherwise employees will feel under pressure. Sometimes it is good to not have a manager of those employees, to enable them to speak openly.

Follow-up
To reconfirm credibility after the meeting all the captures actions should be shared with participants and followed-up until resolved. Otherwise this may create a perception that executives are not that interested.

Newsletters

A Newsletter is a good media to share content with large number of relevant employees. Someone should own preparation of the content and a nice layout. Relevant content for a newsletter could be either update on the transformation journey as well as content on people agenda, i.e. development trainings, workshops, opening of new roles, etc.

6.10. SUPPORTING THE NEW ORGANIZATION

It will take some time while the new function or department or organization will be in an operational mode and most probably there will be challenges during the ramp up phase. Some of those challenges may include but are not limited to:

- Lack of clarity about the scope of the work;
- Not all roles are filled;
- Need some time to build up a working and cooperating mode;
- Higher expectations from internal customer.

Change management should be done also during the newly created organization during the ramp up period.

Some ideal to be considered for that purpose are listed below:

- Conduct more frequent internal customer satisfaction surveys focused on the key services of the new organization. The survey can be conducted quarterly or even monthly and will be a good basis to understand the direction in which things are developing. There is no need to create a comprehensive satisfaction survey this these purposes: just a few key questions will help to understand the trend.
- End-to-end process walkthrough. If a new organization is created to drive the whole process or part of it, there may be some interface and scope issues. Therefore, a good idea may be to bring together managers overseeing all steps of one process and holistically reviewing the process, gaps, interfaces, inputs and outputs.
- MNCs have global departments, and if a transformation impacted or created a global department, then we must put focus on virtual team management and leadership in a virtual environment.

7. SUSTAINING THE TRANSFORMATION

Post transformation - how to sustain the new state to get lasting benefits?

Ideally transformation culture should become a process from a project. The processes should have owners who should strive to improve all process steps, and make process leaner, etc. One of the ways to sustain implemented changes is to take ownership of the end-to-end process, which has changed. One of the ways to do so is business process management. Let us have a look at that. Per Theodore Panagacos, Business process management (BPM) is a field in operations management that focuses on improving corporate performance by managing and optimizing a company's business processes. As a managerial approach, BPM sees processes as strategic assets of an organization that must be understood, managed, and improved to deliver value-added products and services to clients.

If a new process had been set up, then it makes sense to introduce key performance indicators to measure the effectiveness and efficiency of the new process. The stakeholders of the process should be consulted on those KPIs and should regularly receive an update on KPI actual data from the process owner.

A qualitative approach to sustain changes is to periodically conduct surveys from the stakeholders as well as sounding board meetings or calls with selected representatives of stakeholder groups. Team members from internal customer and service department should put together and urged to work on some current topics to jointly come up with a resolution. This will help to increase trust and one team spirit.

8. CONCLUSION

Performance of the corporation is significantly impacted by the employee engagement. When a corporation needs to transform, this impact gets even higher. Employee engagement is the soft component of transformation and change management includes actions to focus on it to help transformation be successful and allowing a corporation to enjoy its intended benefits. This can be done through understanding of different levels of change impact on employees, creation of strategy during transformation, and focusing on the quantity of positive activities which will eventually turn into quality.

9. APPENDIX 1 – WHY TRANSFORMATION FAILS

There are multiple reasons why transformation can fail, but the following ones are key from my perspective:

- No clear strategy/ objective / timeline set for transformation
- No alignment among leadership team
- No support from the local/impacted leaders
- Lack of communications and interaction with employees
- No focus on people agenda and support of impacted employees
- Losing talents to other companies

10. APPENDIX 2 – EXAMPLES OF ACTION PLANS

Action plan for Transformation Manager.

#	Description
1	Familiarize with available umbrella/top-down/global resources on the strategy and storyline
2	Work with global team to plan and conduct necessary meetings or workshops in the area of responsibility
3	Conduct regular status update sessions with impacted leaders and human resources department
4	Regularly provide status update and upward feedback to global or guiding transformation team
5	Support impacted leaders to conduct meetings or calls for impacted employees in the relevant country or department
6	Support impacted leaders in preparing material pack and support in presenting it to internal or external customers of impacted leaders
7	Act as a single point of contact about transformation and resulting changes for all impacted employees
8	Ensure that 1:1 communication takes place between each impacted employee and manager

	to discuss and align what transformation means for each employee
9	Monitor employee engagement and customer satisfaction rates
10	Identify key players who may be at list of leaving country, department, or company
11	If employee's role may disappear, support manager in preparing individual action plan for each impacted employee, i.e. new role in same or other department, other country, newly created role, upskilling or training.
12	Develop a draft post-transformation organization structure

Action plan for Employee.

#	Description
1	Read available materials and attend sessions and workshops to understand why transformation is happening and what is the plan
2	Attend specific sessions set up by transformation team to deep dive into transformation
3	Work with manager and transformation manager, and human resources department to understand how your role is impacted due to transformation.
4	Together with manager and transformation manager, create an individual action plan (i.e. no action, up-skilling or training, looking for new role, etc.)
5	Support transformation team in conducting the transformation, i.e. work shadowing, change of activities., etc.
6	Provide constructive feedback to manager, transformation manager, and transformation team on what can be done better
7	Stay positive and have fun

www.ingramcontent.com/pod-product-compliance
Lightning Source LLC
Chambersburg PA
CBHW022100170526
45157CB00004B/1414